Good, Clean Mania: Collected Poems 2020-2022

Good, Clean Mania: Collected Poems 2020-2022

Good, Clean Mania: Collected Poems 2020-2022

Jasper Ezekiel

Published by Jasper Ezekiel, 2023.

GOOD, CLEAN MANIA: COLLECTED POEMS 2020-2022

First edition. June 9, 2023.

Copyright © 2023 Jasper Ezekiel.

ISBN: 979-8223871200

Written by Jasper Ezekiel.

Table of Contents

This book is dedicated to my late friend, a fellow poet, J de Salvo. Rest in peace, J, you should be publishing this book.

The cover is a self protrait by the poet. The back cover is a linocut illustration of "my cat sees clearer than i" by Lucien King.

A List of Symptoms Followed by the Cure
2020

1

A Drinking Game To Accompany This Work
- Take a shot when I make you crave a cigarette.
- Take a shot when you wonder who my poem is about.
- Take a shot when you mistake past lovers for new.
- Take a shot when I make you happy you'll never be me.
- Take a shot when I mention the seasons.
- Take a shot when I remind you of a natural disaster.
- Take a shot when I remind you life goes on.
If you played this game take another shot when you finish the book so you can read it in the morning for the first time again.

Ass Blasted into the Fourth Dimension

I drift with the mint flavored vape clouds up to the light polluted sky to the barely visible stars, hopping from one to the other like stones in a rushing stream. From up here I can see you praying to a God who has only told you to hurt yourself, a holy figure closer to Satan with the blood He's instructed you to spill. How can we submit to God's Plan if we can't know what He wants? Prayer left me psychotic and lonely, my tongue wrapped tightly around a language only I could understand. Prayer left me blindfolded and trusting, God holding His hand out for me, only inches out of reach.

In the stars I find an uncomfortable isolation. Something I grew up with, unwanted just the same. I learned to expect no response when I speak. I learned my cries receive no soothing touches, no care, no affection. No animals are in the stars to keep me company. Heaven is still so far above me. I can't make out the silhouette of the Gates, only darkness for miles. But I hear the party booming, the pounding beat. Below me, you must hear it too, it's why you pray. I hope you aren't praying for selfish things like people often do, I hope you pray for courage, strength, patience, serenity.

I pray for the stars to fall into your cupped hands, to blaze and burn the flesh to your bone.

I pray for you to ignore the way I look at you, to see nothing behind my eyes, to know I am not a threat.

And most of all I pray for you to be happy, with your human craving and your addict obsession with anything that gives you pleasure.

I would hate you if you wrote about me like this. I don't have a justification. I have my obsession. I scrape this scum off my soul to make art. I take my dirtiness and I show it to God and He turns the sweat off my hot, embarrassed cheeks into wine and when I offer decadence to you, you turn it down and say, "No thanks, I've had enough."

The Man in the Red Hat

The voice in my head sounds like yours
Sounds like chainsmoker
Sounds like God lives in your throat holds back a flood of obscenity

"I fucked her," you tell me. "Oh, how I fucked her"

For the most part you keep your hands to yourself
Sometimes you touch her like she's an angel
She'll bruise your shaking hands
Her bones will explode through her flesh and embed in your body like
shrapnel

I think about crawling into her skin to feel your hands around my throat
To grow my hair out so you'll corner me in a dark kitchen
While I try to run from the party

"I'll fuck you," you'll say. "Oh, how I'll *fuck* you"

I hide behind your homophobia
You see through my masculinity front
And when I speak you thank me for my transparency
Turn your head towards her
Move on

Love Letter to The One Winged Angel That Lived Parasitically In My Unconscious Thoughts

i rejected my mother when i had long hair
and hid androgynous in the back
of my creative writing classes
i disregarded reality
and abandoned individuality in favor of
becoming one with my twinky high school boyfriend

bleaching his hair on his balcony
he complains that it burns
and i have to explain that was normal
after he washes his hair it isn't platinum the way he wants it
there are blisters on his ears
skin red
like his face when i go down on him
to sooth the pain

i have lunch with mother
my invisible angel wings weigh heavy on my back
while i eat expensive crepes and ice cream
a well balanced meal while i look across the table at her
think about apologizing for having sex in her house when she told me
you're too young to be doing those things
and Anne Rice should never have written Interview With A Vampire
because it's giving you weird ideas about homosexuality

i shave my head
i break up with my boyfriend

i wear drag to class
i pretend to be a wizard
it's fall
i drink
my mother says she loves me

in my bathroom i bleach my buzzcut
when i wash the bleach out my scalp is stained
with flaking chemical burns
and my hair looks invisible, so light

Decaf Coffee at Midnight

There is an unrest in the dark parts of my soul
Where I hide my politics and all the bad karma
My body has yet to repay
"We don't have a static self," my friend always says
But I haven't been changing
And it's a misquote anyway
So none of it matters
I break quarantine to wander my neighborhood and smoke cigarettes
And everyone else is breaking quarantine too
With their dogs and their boyfriends
And their little kids
They cross the street when they see me
Everyone is scared
But me most of all
Because I want to write and I want to quit smoking
But I can't
I want to stay up all night and do nothing
But I won't
I brew decaf coffee at midnight
While my phone lays dead in front of me
(I've been ignoring all those I owe my life to)
I drink decaf coffee at midnight
And my inaction leads to discontent
And my imagined action leads to discontent
And the dark parts of my soul grow
And I do nothing

Eleven Eleven

I wish it could be 11:11 forever so I could sit in the magic of thinking of what my wish would be

I wish to circumvent mania and learn how to cope
To fall into the destined stability of my thirties
Even though bipolar is never cured
The mountainous moods turn into bumps in the road
Or so they say

I wish for the time before cigarettes
Days in my room with no call to outdoors
No cravings, no sickness
No pressure headaches
Do I wake up with sore lungs because I smoke half a pack a day?
Or is it because of the blossoming flowers, bright white outside my window?

I wish for a better life
A skinnier body, a bigger cock
I wish for my love to be local
I wish to be productive
I wish

And it takes too long for me to think of a wish
It's 11:12
It's not like wishing will change anything
But maybe through angel number magic
And force of will
Things will be set right

My Favorite Red T Shirt With A 3 Eyed Satanic Goat On It

The pipes are backed up
I thought I would have to sacrifice my clothes to the shit smell
That flooded with sewage into the washing machine
When you offered to buy me new t shirts
My image crafted by your hand
I wanted them to be ruined
Just for the thrill of starting over
To have you shape my new beginning
My clothes are in the dryer
The smell is gone from the garage
But I'm afraid to check them
Just in case
The smell remains
And my metamorphosis is catalyzed
By faulty plumbing

When He Killed The Goddess, I Wept At Her Grave Until Her Eyes Glowed And She Breathed Again

I go to write a letter to him
For my poets tendencies to write letters to people
Long dead
(Be it physical
Or metaphorical)
And I found I had nothing to say
No "fuck you"
No "how could you"
No "I demand an apology"
Just a slight discomfort at his ghost
Like the pain as a splinter is removed
The skin healing
To its original shape
If I were to ever meet him
Touring the university in Northridge with my friend
Or if I simply find myself in LA
I would hope
He has nothing to say to me

Nicotine Addicts Don't Have Much To Write About

You thought I was your lover when really I was the cigarette
you shared with me on the bridge connecting Oakland and Emeryville
after a little kid called us faggots at the Barnes and Noble in the open air
mall too rich to have a hot topic

Really I was the cigarette
you bought me as I ran away from my parents while we were out of state
that you could buy because the legal smoking age was lower there and it
was just one cigarette what could it hurt you knew I missed smoking pot
so you said smoke this instead

Really I was the cigarette
untouched in the pack I gave you your expensive brand I just wanted
to see you smile reaching across your car after the pandemic had started
even though we sat unmasked only inches from each other while you
drove me home

Really I was the cigarette
in your shaking drunk hand relapsing now two weeks off heroin you told
me the apple was a gift from the fallen angel that god was your father was
the president was the patriarchy and it all made sense to me but you said
I'm sorry I'm just so drunk and laughed it all off like you'd just told me a
joke

Really I was the cigarette
I was smoking on the curb across the street from my house so I won't
disturb my parents when the smoke drifts in through their open
bedroom window thinking about how much I miss you even though you

don't understand a word I say, no shared tongue, only wild gestures and condemning faces and a distance between us larger than galaxies

Mania or Ambition?

Up all night
Meditation
In the yard
I have to climb out my window
To enter my secret garden
God waits for me there
And says
"Everything will be okay"

8/19/20

Another forest fire
Tearing through Northern California
I smoke so I'm not worried about the AQI
But I see it, red, screenshotted on my Twitter feed
By a concerned journalist
She says "stay inside and stay safe"
I worry
About pregnant woman without N-95s forced to grocery shop by workaholic husbands
And homeless people breathing in the fumes
But what's new?
I always worry
About those less fortunate than me
We all wear masks now
When we can

"The normal amount of fires are zero"
my boyfriend says over text when I show him
The Twitter screenshots of clouds of red and yellow
But it's been common for years now
The air unbreathable from August to October
I worry
About cancers and evacuations
Millions of dollars in property damage
Whatever that means
But what's new?
I always worry
Because there's always something
To fucking worry about

After the Psychosis

I stare at the reflection in the train window
as we drive under the bay my hair is in my eyes and I look derelict
tired ass dressed in black holey sweatshirt and black fingerless knit gloves
the shittiest facial hair growing in on my neck and my jaw
but not my cheeks or my lips

San Francisco used to be magical
after I stopped getting stoned it turned into a city full of concrete
steaming vents
tourist trap pier 49 San Francisco
used to be the center of my universe
even though I only visited.

in a daze to walk and walk in a manic fit
trying to calm my beating heart and outrun government spies
the lights on the Bay bridge showed me the next Messiah
his face becomes my death mask
as I succumb without struggle to the joys of ego death

The Only Constellation I Recognize

I walk barefoot through the broken glass on my street
It melts beneath the heat of my skin like ice
Whenever I'm alone I think 'I could get used to this'
But I always end up missing you
Even if you lived in California
You would be asleep by now
Just yesterday the moon was full
But now she's hiding her face from me
Turned away in shame
Maybe
To see her son nestled between trash cans
With a cigarette between his lips
I always wonder if you'll mind the smell
I like to be awake long enough
To see Orion's belt in the Winter sky
The only constellation in the sky I recognize
When I meet you my heart will sing with recognition
The same I feel when
I imagine standing on that hot star
That shows in Earth's cold sky next to the moon
I'll take your hand
And I'll tell you
"I always knew you were home to me"

Good, Clean Mania
2021

Maw In the Rockface

It always starts with my teeth
Shining brightly in the dark
The blinding light is uncomfortable
The blinding light is pain
I follow it to the first steps on the journey
That I know will only end in regret

But I don't regret
Baring my teeth
It unlocks the first door of the journey
And shines light on my life of darkness
I always knew there would be pain
I have never known comfort

I've been crying to find comfort
I always bring regret
Growth always follows pain
Pain always comes when I grind my teeth
Like earthquake lights in the dark
My stress guides the journey

There is no jubilance as I journey
I find no solace, no joy, no comfort
All that greets me is darkness
On the ground I find loose teeth
And I wonder if they were pulled out of regret
I relish in their imagined pain

But I am in no pain

20

I am simply journeying
From one crooked bite to the next snarled tooth
The white bone comforts
The solace I find as deep as the regret
Of losing a loved one in the dark

I become a creature of the dark
Of rotting things and pain
Through our mock affection I make you regret
Being a part of my journey
I try to take your comfort
I do it with my teeth

It's been a mistake to have you in the cavernous darkness of my journey
I've never felt regret as I caused you pain
My spirit grows into something more comfortable as I use you as
something to teeth on

the only bench in my fiance's apartment complex

city boy in suburban new jersey
sweet taste of something quiet after bracing myself
for landing gear to give way
flying into Newark
to meet my muse for the first time
his big beautiful real body exactly my same height
all hope of him being taller seems silly
when his head rests perfectly on my shoulder
while we make a scene at the luggage pick up
people stare and smile
his kiss tastes like two layers of surgical mask
nicotine lozenge breath in mine

the green bench
hidden in the sea of trimmed grass
sit cross legged for fear of ticks
until my young and aged hips protest
and i risk lyme disease infection

dew covered toes
touch droplets through open sandals
blurry brain and fighting off mania
with lithium salt
dehydrated lips
wishing i had taken a sip
from his giant red water bottle
before I left

despite my wired thoughts
the only bench in his apartment complex
only keeps me supported for so long
his warm body beckons
warmer than summer that brings morning
to a rolling boil
my relaxed muscles absorbing the heat
like metal in the sun

this poem can only be written for long
before i use too many pages
&tear down the rainforest with my love
that lasts forever

yes, there really is a kalamazoo

Sometimes I get like I'm fifteen driving in a rented car to Michigan back when people used to text me holding my phone between my legs as it vibrates with canned replies just to feel loved by somebody

I thought I'd lost someone back then to the sheer cliffside of a land far away but the gravity of loss hadn't occurred to me yet and when I learned I forgot about it for a while until I couldn't anymore.

That trip I laid in the guest bed for two weeks straight and only left to freeze my balls off listening to trumpets in a town square like something from a season's greetings postcard. I had rejected the Bible at that point but I still pretended they were the seventh one and I'd never make it home. But that's not really in the Bible, that's just some guy's shroom trip documented for eternity, right? Who ever heard of a pale horse anyway.

I kept telling people that I'm not me and I gave them all these different names and personas and still no one wanted to fuck me. And no one did for a long time. So I jerked off with my brother in the room and installed and uninstalled Grindr for years until I didn't have to lie about my age any more. And nothing happened then either.

Nostalgia means nothing when you are so miserable the only thing to romanticize is your self harm. Maybe I owe myself an apology. But more realistic: I need to write better poems about it. What's the point of bleeding if you can't slap a glitter filter over it and post that shit to tumblr?

haven't met you yet

lack of sense memory means i only see the ghost of you when i think of
our love
long distance lovers
my favorite phrased as of yet unused in a presentable poem
i sing songs to you when you're thousands of miles away
i imagine you hear me while you wash dogs at work
and sing with me in our joy

when i fall asleep with a rush in my ears
your phone distorted voice echoing through my mind
my head against your chest
your heartbeat
and mine
beating together

four more sleeps now and daddy's a mess
can't sleep barely eating and smoking like an old woman at a slot machine
when i see you i'll stabilize
the way the earth settles after a quake
fall in love with you again
touching you this time
looking into your eyes
instead of an eight month old picture
of your fading red hair and stoned red face
stuffed ducky cuddled where i should be

i have never felt
more certain
about anything in my life

than i do about the concepts of
you
&
forever
spinning round with puffy flowing skirts
until their colors all mesh into one psychedelic rainbow
of certainty
reassuranty
eternity

face hugger survivor support group

I have no connection to this life
Except that night
In his room
Passing the parasite from my mouth to his
And feeling it crawl down the back of my throat
To make a home in my yeast infected cunt

Poems like this are tiring to write
But more exhausting to live

He makes a nest for the birds outside the window
Of the long hair I want to grow
The birds lay eggs that are eaten
By green tree snakes
From beyond this region

Perils of Psychiatry

Numbed on neurontin
Painful psychiatry
Acupuncture to the brain
Poems come like mud through a hose
Oozing out through little needle holes
and leech bites of bloodletting
Psychotic break
Tumbling falling to your doom
Earthquake shake
Predicted by google in my room
If I had known it would have happened
A little ShakeAlert on my phone
For technicolor psychosis
What would I have done?
But then again is that not what my doctor is?
If you don't stop smoking pot
Then...
Threatening me with symptoms
I thought I knew how to control
Loony still on lithium
Rapid response of risperidone
Does it ever stop?
Like the seasons, bipolar comes and goes
And goes and goes and goes

sandy pawprints by the no dogs sign

morning breath and cotton mouth,
dehydrated kisses
on the beach
never seen the sunrise proper
rising on the east
coast
where i come from there's not so much of this
only foggy morning after sleepless night
sand in my shoes as we approach the reflection on the sea
i didn't know how much i longed for
Atlantic ocean
holding your hand
your little black dog
leaving footprints in her toddling wake

hartshorne woods park

I hold your jacket around my waist while you jog ahead with hyperactive
nervous dog
the black dog an inside joke between you and Satan
your little hellhound
hellish for sure

Your scent wafts to me on the winter breeze
temperate and dry
I lick my lips and chew off dead skin
scab and hot soup burn one and the same
allergy red Rudolph nose
and ASMR sniffles

How foolish of me to think I'd leave the dying world with you
we talk until 2 in the morning with the window open
I used to think earthquake weather was reserved for the pacific rim
hot spot of volcano and disaster
but the wind bringing rain
blows in 70 degree ocean fog
Oh, how I miss the still frozen Alaskan melt

I type poetry on my phone
silicon microchip slave labor phone
How can I avoid it when the sun beats down in December?
The dead leaves coat the ground like ice
and ancestor memory of broken bones makes my steps hesitant
I slide down a cliff
and you catch me,
my warm hand in yours

zombie

behind me something lurks
bloated face and drooling lips
dripping acid spit onto the floor
a corpse with my face lays in my bed for me to wake up with in the
morning
something bad will not happen
it is happening now and I see it
in the corner of my vision
absent when I turn to seek it
caricature schizophrenic I look in the mirror
my face snarls at itself and I startle
there is nothing in this world but myself
fractals of a poet reflecting hot rays of skewed psyche
burning hot sun on a mirror
I seer my own ant skin
a hole in each of my palms
and feet
paralyzed I am bedridden
my corpse companion turns to me
to steal my life
and make me waking dead
inhabited by the passed self
wearing me like a cheap leopard print suit

hurray! spring is here!

the pandemic is over
(we say through our masks)
funk music playing fades into rock fades into disco
battle of the bands from one group to
the next to the dj at the impromptu skate park
crossing the street nearly hit by skaters doing tricks
am i just a cone to you?
said flirting with long blond skater boy
skunk and damiana
similar but not quite
one sweeter but which?
the joyous noise of laughter and relief
of suntime again after long winter
sick winter
vaccine spring

youtube child "entertainer"

laughing delirious in child's play place
scraped together shit from leaking anal birth
and shoved into suspenders and propellor cap
primary color blinder to soul so rotten it's only dust
remnants of a man once full of life
he straddles the swings and rocks
back and forth
torpedo caterpillar green and blue
he descends into disease ridden pit
to play with balls and count them
one two three
children scream for attention for plushie animatronic blippi
ignored and shunned and pushed down the slide
head first into play foam carpets
while camera crews look on
while children at home, mommy in the other room, look on
algorithms play
lost and tired man
exploiting children and ai
for a buck
playing next: stupid girl gets caught in chuck e cheese slide
thumbnail: ass, panties showing, no head, only legs

Nature Calls

In the deserted California forest
Not the redwoods but close by
Bare legs scratched by underbrush stickers
Tumbling down a hill made of the threat of poison oak
But it's a well maintained trail
And I wasn't so scared of bugs yet
Maybe it was the way May still looked like March and how when I settled down
On a tree stump by the trail in a patch of grass
My body cooled down and I was suddenly shivering again

I brought my backpack
Full of munchies and my water bottle best friend
Tap water and ice
It sweat onto my notebooks and bled the poetry inside
Little plastic vibrator
With a knob at the bottom to crank it up

Jeans undone legs spread on the stump
Little whimpers
Upon completion a man jogged by and said, "Good afternoon"
"Hi "
And he was on his way

Forbidden exhibitionism giggling making myself up
Finger-combing hair and wiping vibrator off on my shirt
Body warm again
I sat there and I ate

34

Long hike back
Harder uphill
and a bus ride for hours
The engines sounded like they sang

my sad attempt at vulture culture

bodies not buried in my backyard
bones macerating in pools of Tupperware
stolen from mom's cupboard
of course I didn't tell her
squirrel found on way back from work
stop by for rubber gloves
and garbage bag
dad threw out my bones
connection to the other side
the psychic vulture in me wept that day
for necklaces and rituals unborn
maybe one day again
I'll find the perfect corpse
of rodents not yet eaten
but it hasn't happened in a while
lithium salts the bones I lost
and they dry to brittle cracking
crumbling like ashes in the wind

pennsylvania it is

the darkest it's ever been
in the Pennsylvania forest
drunk and the porch light goes out
you wait for me inside

oakland night

moon showing down
through front yard beach umbrella
of only if were so simple
to close it and see her

the technicolor awakening of the psychedelic spirit on that night far from home

Psychedelic or psychotic lifetimes
I said I was blue when you told me I was acting red
But I was having an awakening
When I walked with you that night
Far away from home
You looked inside and saw my spirit

Spirit ecstatic, drastic change of
the nature of psychdelia
Among the stars I found my home
The Zodiac written in fire-orange
Across the sky that night
They called to me in Aquarius awakening

Awakening from a sleep unslept
The manic buzz of particles, my spirit cried
Days blurred with endless night
Tripping forever, stuck and psychedelic
The sun was lemon yellow
Blinding me from my the windows in my home

At home I stayed until the flood passed
Asleepening with no sleep and waking with no awakening
The trees outside were blinding green
And my muted aura stayed subdued spirit
I was sick of psychedelic
And the neverending soul night

The night was when the raccoons came to find me
As I sat and smoked cigarettes outside of my home
Disillusion with the spirit realm of colors psychedelic
Through illusion I unsaw my awakening
And in my body, withered my spirit
Finally I came back to myself and was blue again

Indigo then, months of sadness
I denied myself the comfort of the night
There was no more spirit
Anxiety and the world faded from outside my home
I had fallen asleep again and undone my awakening
Those saying 'psychotic' drowned out my psychedelic

But I grew and back came my psychedelic, unburied my awakening, and
found in the stars again my home
I was overcome with violet, accepting into my blood the night and shone
again my spirit

baby's first thunderstorm

in california lightning brings
blazing trauma
not beautiful in the moment for fear of the fire
here i hold your hand at night
while fireflies between drops of rain dance at the edges of my vision
the storm approaches
and for now the water drips through some kind of pine
into my hair you brushed back into a high ponytail
occasionally you take your hand to light your pipe
your dog grunts
and lightning flashes
countless bolts across the sky
this is what i'll remember to write poetry about
to come back to when i've left
memory stored in resin
healthy recall
to assist in long distance
thunder rolls
and i kiss you
to ask you to protect me from the divine

in the suburban park surrounded by freeway

the sunset is hidden by unprecedented fog
it reminds me driving up into the hills back home
buzzed in the middle of the night
in california we throw our cigarette butts into the high fire risk straw
grass on the side of the road
but here we drop them into a bottle full of rotten chocolate protein shake
consumed to stop my starving belly from passing gas after 8 hours in the
plane
when i leave you'll hold onto the bottle long after i've gone
i know this because you joked about it the same way we used to joke
about getting married

despite the hidden sunset you take me out into the dark woods and the
phantom flash of a fox i saw earlier haunts my anxious mind but nothing
happens except us looking at the fireflies and the fog amplifying the
sound of our kisses

when the car starts our song starts playing where we left off and i forget
the annoyance i felt when you turned the car off half an hour ago in the
middle of it. we hold hands while you drive and over and over i tell you
about how beautiful the fireflies were in the dark in the deep suburban
new jersey

God & Love & My Dead Cat
2022

infinite(simal)

i touch ur leg - u in front of me in my mind - and my hand touches ur
hairy shin with a gentle touch, ` glide, car e s s .

u may think that i am touching u but there is an infinite space between
each skin flake,
hair follicle, coagulated red blood cell hidden under ur bright blue
bandaid.

the data stored inside of each of us has to travel through vectors
unthinkable before coming scrambled into my heart.

    u take my hand.

        'the word yr thinking of is infini*tesimal*,' u say.

my palms sweat with exertion and shake slightly thinking of those poor
atoms, my poor heart, so close but still not quite touching. i know what i
said but yr right.
what i think is space unending is so small it can't be understood.

    but space nonetheless.

i give u ur victory, for i have enacted syntax sins.
to make it up to u, i guess i'll just have to spend the rest of my life trying
to disregard science and touch in a magic embrace of fourth dimension
love infinite,

    infinitesimal,

indeniable.

airport aubade

the alarm goes off at 3:00 in the morning
summer morning
still cold
we walk on tiptoe
not to wake your mother asleep on the couch

dunkin' donuts brown sugar cold brew foam from the drive through
gray sunrise clouds still accented dark in whirls of fog
didn't sleep much stomach ache
and menthol cigarettes one after another in your car

you drove me to the airport but I wish I had left you
sleeping under well loved comforter
I hope your bed isn't too warm by my heat when you collapse back there
alone
I wish
you could have slept more and I could sacrifice myself
for your wellness
but without a license i rely on your insomnia winds
to carry me, dreading, to the gate

we press our masks together before security
the taste of synthetic polymer
instead of your always dry lips
you go home without me
on your way before the plane leaves

on my layover I drink three beers and text you
so alone and full of regret that they can take me into the back

and mold me into mystery meat
to serve as an overpriced burger

Self Portrait as an Angel

I.
and the sky opened up and God said,
thunderclap and lightning, unintelligible words from above!
from the din, one angel borne from the wreckage of a heavenly civil war
as pink and gooey as the day he was "born".

infantile angel
his heart bleeds sanguine sap,
blues and reds swap color for lack of a better solution
to hide the gold of ichor running.
silver spell of trauma in dream world
pain & weapon unheard
silent in face of fragile psyche.

poor angel,
child angel,

      layers of angel
      peeled away

until no angel left.

pure sensory being.
colors speak like voices,
pain thrum beat
drum ringing in the ears.

II.
one day he doesn't sleep.

a day is any other day when all the days feel the same pull and tug of manic depressive mood swings, like tides spitting mountains of crabs scuttling from the deep subconscious onto the shore of his mind
and the nights stretch on and on into endless darkness of shadow creatures reaching claws out sharpened on the stone of his resolve to never give into their whisperings
the angel, unsleeping, traveled across the globe to chase the sunrise after sunrise like a storm only to be greeted by the relentless dawn after dawn after dawn

until he realized that, when it came down to it, it was the day he couldn't run from, not the sun.

so he sits on top of a mountain and the sun rises, noon brings trickle of melted snow through the day, wet through to dead frostbitten skin, spring sunset panic attack soothes eventually into the the path of the milky way.

the full moon was like a perfect synchronicity, or maybe He planned it that way. the moon lites the valleys below in milky pools

    & grass peeks little heads out through the snow.

Solitary Sex Magic

I fall into the arm of white plastic,
Bliss of vibrations sweet, turn up, turn down,
Body contorts in shapes acrobatic
I get so high I hope I won't come down.

Imagine him here, he wouldn't know why
I hide myself beneath the blankets.
I turn away from him, so hot and so shy
then I reveal myself to explain it.

Though now I spend my nights in bed alone,
My lover will soon give companionship.
For now I have what I have always known:
A magic wand held in my trembling grip.

When he's away I feel isolated
but for now at least I've masturbated.

munditia

inspired by professor miller

"full body relic.
brown shirt bikers
& old old ladies
go to this church.
the whole world is turning protestant
but *bavaria*
exhumes the bodies of saints from the catacombs!
bejeweled martyr,
in her chalice is a dead bird.
sadly no one will tell me why."

Vindication is the Best

On a busy Sunday afternoon,
at a hardware store called Ace,
I wrongly thought I was immune
to the stressors of the place.

A man was having a pretty bad day,
as retail employees are wont to do.
He had the audacity to say
something that made my vision a red hue.

He said, "I don't care what color
you're deciding on!
Make your mind up, brother,
so we can get a move on."

I pondered his remark
and decided he was rude.
"I was trying to tell you 'something dark'
if you had the patience to hear me, dude."

My dad tried to save face
and hurried me out the door.
The man called out as we left the place,
"What the hell did i mix this for??"

Dad went back inside and paid
While I waited by the car.
He was embarrassed, upset, dismayed.
I would have walked home if it weren't too far.

Back home, dad told me, "It was a busy Sunday,
that man was tired and mad.
I reckon he'd had a long day
there was no reason for fighting to be had."

We got to work in the room
and as we painted to to the night,
we opened our second can of paint
only to find that it was white.

"It was a busy Sunday afternoon,"
I reminded my dad in jest.
He mumbled about the stupid goon...
Vindication is the best!

red sunset over sf bay

sent pictures to my fiance and my best friend
to no answer due to time zones and single mother responsibilities
they'll see it soon
and wish they were here with me

silhouette of the marin hills
layers of black obscure fire summer sunset
coast guard helicopter drills over the water
adds another layer to quiet symphony of
wind blown grass
gentle touch of water against the stones beneath us
mom and dad talking in the distance while the dog softly woofs

i wish i could paint
i'd paint spider web red sun reflection on blue blue water

bird flies across my field of vision
still like a toy as it glides
with wings unmoving
on the cooling breeze

moon peeks out finally over wispy clouds
thumbnail crescent bright
like a hole in the sky
that shows the other side

the wet blue funk

at first i think it's raining when i step outside
you texted me this morning before you left for work that there were
4 weeks until i see you again
this creeping anxiety is soothed by the cold humidity

i remember when i first saw you
in july
i woke up early for class the day before
and outside while i smoked
little droplets were in the air like fairies
how can it be raining in june? i thought
that doesn't happen around here
you explained the concept to 22 year old me
this california boy didn't know about humidity it seems
until i felt it like little blisters popping on my skin

there's nothing to do but wait
and watch the condensation on the window
burn as the sun rises
distracted as i always am by you

farewell party

the rain salutes us off

goodbye sun soaked hippie
drunk on light and true love
sitting on the outskirts of the party
looking for something to smoke
keep his mouth occupied from spilling secrets
of their escape route

goodbye gentle metalhead
stoned on farewell parties
that last hit on the bong he shared
with best friend for life
the bong they shared now hers forever
unable to fit it in the suitcase with the rest of his life inside
parting gift of one last smoke sesh
goodbye, goodbye, goodbye

reflection cast in bubble raindrop
blown off the windshield
back to the atlantic

rising sun comes up fast
that day as they drive towards the sunrise
towards blue skies
and pop punk on the radio

Mercy I

nuns habit burned in summer bonfire
Christ-child let's ashes mark his forehead in inverted cross
charred hot skin from live coals
and little embers.

mom's nightgown swallows him up like a baby hiding in the sheets
in the backyard warm breeze blows billows of sweet comfort sunheat.
the gown is white purity
until Christ-child puts it on & fabric runs red with postbirth bleeding
gone on for years now.
he takes it off at the altar
at night his husband lays claim to his broken body
his seed settles inside to conceive another antichrist
the first red and squealing baby not enough.

Christ-child prays in the morning.
Mary, if you're there, deliver me from myself.
dry my cunt and warm my heart.
still my hand when my husband comes near
and bleed my throat to deny him.
Mary never answers.

Satan fills the void
delivers unto sin.
is the body of the wicked ways.
soaks the cunt.
grasps with hands.
and opens the throat for his husband.

blackened heart and squealing, Satan fills Christ-child's light
leaves him dark in the hopeless dawn.

Mercy II

released from the convent,
chest hair grows in sparse fields of wheat after the famine.
he's allowed now to lounge in shorts,
shorn hair not enough to hide sun-kissed scalp,
sweat refracted sunburn.

he finds his mother's nightgown in a trunk under the bed.
when the washing is done, he hides his tiny body in the backyard
warm breeze blows billowing white sheets.
lacy gown swallows knob knees, grassy bare feet bleeds congealed jelly.
the detergent smell, the drying rain, mom's baking after dinner.

Future Bible Heroes Playing Over a Speaker in the Mall

I dreamed he towered over me again one night
skinny in his plush black coat,
smiles with those small, narrow eyes.

We ate in a food court,
dipped greasy fries into acid ketchup
and talked with our mouths full in the joy of each other's company.
He stood to leave
but I chased him outside
where I stopped him and he put out his arms.
I embraced him.

"I don't want to wake up," I said.
"Because I know you won't be there."

He had no language left,
(spirits rarely speak,)
but he held me and it was as if it was in waking,
the smell of cigarettes,
smoke shop incense
and cheap laundry detergent
tangled in the acrylic fabric of his fake fur coat.

When I woke up, I thought about making plans with him before I
remembered.

Some weeks I dream of him every night. I feel him when I talk about
him. I know he's reading this poem. Hi there. I hope you don't feel like

I'm using you to make my art better. If that's the case, I'm sorry. But you're a poet too. I hope you'll understand and embed yourself into these words to haunt the reader like you haunt me.

When You Dream About Someone It Means They Have Something to Say to You

God comes in vibrations over my body in the everlit forest,
like an album cover or a well-lit twilight in an otherwise problematic
movie.
The glow consumes, post orgasm shock and wet eyes.
The tears come out crystalized, Christ-relics
in the palm of my swelling hand.

In the forest, there is a bowl of rice waiting for me.
A test.
The steam from it is illuminated in a sunbeam - orange as it sets.
The bowl, made of stone, is raised for me. I know He left it.

Hungry as I am, with my hands I take half,
the swell of a mound above the rim of the bowl
and leave it on the ground.
How proud I am to leave an offering for my Father.
How warm the rice is on my tongue,
how it never burns my hands or sticks to my skin as I eat like a beast.

Thank you, I say. A little prayer.
And please receive my offering on this day.
The bounty that I found should be all yours
but greedy human stomachs
and grubby human mouths
swallow half of it down
starving.

Sun sets into misty night.

Prayers cast into the heavens.
Onwards travel to the mountain.

why me

when it rains i always think why me?
why can't I get over it? and
what really happened that made me love him?

my poetry teacher said
no more break-up poems
so, i broke up with break up poems
and grieved that trauma too

blank sheets of paper are poetry
until they're torn in half
then they become two poems
beating hearts
divided forever
by hurting hands
unable to express what's inside

my inner heterosexual

as i bit into the mentos i got to soothe the violent man my father enacted his intergenerational bullshit on i realized this version of myself never wrote much poetry and to him the mento was the most striking feeling worthy of artistic revery.

it wasn't the sharp taste to offset hours of syrupy jolly ranchers that left his mouth dry that got to him.

it wasn't the shape, like a shattered pebble on his quivering tongue.

it was the way that, with some pressure, the hard candy molded to his teeth and softened into something chewable.

he devoured it with mouth gaping, showed the world his conquest of candy. he let me sit his anxious body down for a moment to let me tell him I'm sorry for putting him in such a small box and that I'm glad he's not smoking right now.

my oral fixation, my clenched fist, my reddened face, my hangover. anger has a place in all our hearts.

remembering an outdoor cat

they brought my kitty home in a box
with green leaves and purple flowers
swathes of lavender
sweet smell and a watercolor painting

when the neighbor said they had a dead one
i asked what color
black and white?
kind of skinny?

her face was thrown back to look up at me
a little blood around her mouth
but Ollie all the same
her eyes squinted like when i pet her so hard
her skin got pulled back
and she smiled tiny teeth
tiny red teeth

i always felt so guilty for letting her out
i thought about all those documentaries about mass extinctions
piles of little dead birds in the tweety morgue
i guess i never thought about unfamiliar hands petting her gently
eyes squinting and rumble purr

all the neighbors that slowly dispersed
while my husband held my tears
told me they knew her well
they told me they loved her too

my cat sees clearer than i

second story window
cat sits on the sill
looking at the moonglow
contemplative and still

i wonder what she's seeing
as she's about to leap
it seems we're disagreeing
about when it's time to sleep

i'll close the window on her
when it's time to shut my eyes
i wish that i could warn her
so it isn't a surprise

i see what she had seen
when i get her out of there
leaves of night-washed green
and full moon bright and fair

if i hadn't took down my curtains
i'd never have seen the night
and now i know for certain
that there always is a light

About the Author

Jasper Ezekiel is a young, queer poet from the Bay Area. He is happy to share his heart with the world for the first time. In his free time, he mostly does a wide variety of fiber crafts like knitting, crochet, and handspinning. He has been published before in *The Berkeley Times*, *Milvia Street*, and *Pedestrian Press*.

Read more at https://jasperezekiel.com.